Big Brother is a Gift

Every superhero needs a sidekick. Guess what? ***You just got one!***

Surprise Bonus Inside!

This book includes a special bonus - a fun activity that helps older siblings connect even more with their baby brother or sister. It's a little extra to make this big adventure even more magical

If you enjoy this book, please consider leaving a quick review - your feedback helps other families find and enjoy these stories too!

Table of Contents

Introduction: Welcome to the Big Brother Adventure!

Becoming a BIG BROTHER

Hi! If you are holding this book in your hands, it means that something very important is happening in your home. Soon, or maybe quite recently, someone new appeared - a little brother or sister. And you know what? That means you've just become a big brother!

But wait... What does it actually mean to be an older brother?

First of all, it means that you are more important now than ever before! Your new siblings don't know anything yet, and you can already do a lot of things. You can run, talk, build castles out of blocks, and even tell jokes! Now someone would like to learn all this from you. Sounds cool, right?

What's so special about being a big brother?

Being an older brother is like becoming a superhero - seriously! From now on, you are your siblings' first, most important friend. You will show your toddler how the world works and teach him to play, laugh, and help others. And the best part is that everything you do becomes important to your younger siblings.

The superpowers you didn't know you had:

- Super Patience - the ability to endure even when the toddler screams the loudest in the world.
- Mega Humor - only you know how to make your toddler laugh in any situation.
- Brotherly Courage - From now on, you are the first defender when something goes wrong.
- The Power of Friendship - you are someone your toddler can always count on, even if they can't say it yet.

These stories are just there to make you discover how wonderful it is to be an older brother.

How will these stories help you in your adventure?

In this book, you'll find 15 short stories that will help you see what it's like to have younger siblings. Each story will show you something new - sometimes it will be hilarious, sometimes it will be a little strange, and sometimes it will be quite touching. One thing is sure - you will learn that being an older brother is a real gift and the coolest adventure that could have happened to you.

<u>So, how ready are you for your big adventure? Start!</u>

Part 1: The Big Change - Getting Used to Life with a New Baby

BIG BROTHER
The Great Playground of Patience
The Land of Loud Crying
Valley of Drool
Snack Time Swamp
Mount Pillowfort
Diaper Volcano
The Giggle Garden
The Hall of Hugs
N
W
E
S
Mission: become the best BIG HUGS

1. The Mystery of the Lost Bear

Once upon a time, in a cozy house full of colorful toys and cheerful sounds, lived Jake - a boy with eyes shining like two buttons and a head full of amazing ideas. Jake was the older brother and had a superpower: he could solve puzzles faster than anyone else! He could find a lost sock under the couch, find a brick in the biggest mess, and once even figure out who was snacking on canned cookies (it was Dad, but shhh, it's a secret!). But everything has changed at home for a few weeks because Lily - his little sister - has appeared.

Lily was so tiny that she fit comfortably on a single pillow. She didn't speak yet, but she could laugh like a little bell and cry so loud that you could hear her all the way in the yard. What she loved most in the world was her teddy bear - brown, soft, with one ear a little bigger than the other. Teddy had funny black eyes and always looked like he was smiling. Lily took him everywhere: to her crib, for a walk in the stroller..., and once, she even wanted to bathe him in a bowl of water! But one day something terrible happened - the teddy bear disappeared without a trace!

That afternoon, Jake was sitting in his room, building a huge tower that was out of blocks and could reach the ceiling. Suddenly, he heard a soft sob coming from the next room. It's Lily! He threw the blocks, jumped to his feet, and ran to see what was going on. In the crib, he saw his little sister with a red face

from crying and eyes full of large, round tears. She stretched out her arms as if she wanted to grab something, but there was nothing in her little fists - only an empty place where she usually squeezed the teddy bear.

In the kitchen, Mom and Dad were busy with pots. Mom was cutting carrots, and Dad was mixing something in a big bowl. They both looked tired - they had dark circles under their eyes as if they were drawing them with crayons. When Jake ran in and told about Lily's crying, his mother sighed:

- Jake, maybe you can find her teddy bear? You're so clever, I'm sure you can do it. We have to finish dinner because we will all get hungry.

Jake first thought: "Why always me? I wanted to build a tower!"

But then he looked at Lily, who was still sobbing, and something twitched in him. He felt like a detective from fairy tales, the one who goes on to solve mysteries.

"Okay, I'll find that teddy bear!" he said loudly, clenching his fists and going in search of it.

First, he looked under Lily's crib. It was dark and a bit scary there, but Jake was brave. He found only two tiny polka-dot socks, an old rattle, and a puff of dust that looked like a little grey monster. Teddy was not there.

"Hmmm," Jake muttered and scratched his head.

"Where else could he have hidden?"

He ran to the toy basket in the corner of the room. Inside there was a lot of treasures: colorful balls, a doll with one eye, a plastic toy car without a wheel. Jake turned everything upside down, but there was no trace of the teddy bear! He was beginning to worry.

"What if the bear ran away? Or someone kidnapped him?" - he thought, but then he laughed because teddy bears don't walk alone, do they?

He sat down on the carpet to think. He closed his eyes and imagined that he was a teddy bear.

"If I was plush and small, where would I hide?" he wondered.

Suddenly, he opened his eyes and looked around the room. He noticed that the wardrobe door was slightly ajar.

"Aha!" he shouted, with his heart beating faster.

He ran to the closet and looked inside.

Downstairs, between mom's sweaters and dad's slippers, there was the teddy bear! He was a little dusty and squashed, but it was definitely him, with that funny ear and black eyes. Jake grabbed it and pulled it out triumphantly.

"I've got you!" he cried.

It turned out that Lily, playing with throws, accidentally threw the teddy bear into the closet and then forgot about it. Jake dusted the stuffed animal, straightened its ears, and ran back to his sister.

When Lily saw her friend, her face lit up like the sky after a storm. She stopped crying, stretched out her hands, and hugged the bear so tightly that her curls shook. Jake looked at her and smiled broadly.

"See, teddy bear, you can't run away from Lily!" he said quietly.

Then Mom and Dad ran into the room, hearing that the crying had stopped.

- Jake, you are our number one detective! Dad said and ruffled his hair. Thanks to you, Lily is smiling again, and we can finish dinner.

"You're so helpful, son," Mom added and hugged Jake.

Jake looked at his sister, who was cuddling the teddy bear and cooing to him in her own way. The child beamed with pride, as if they had just won a medal.

"It's not so bad to have a little sister at all," he thought.

Yes, sometimes she was loud, and his parents had less time, but helping Lily made him feel important, like a real big brother.

From that day on, Jake began to look for other ways to help his sister. Sometimes, he brought her a rattle; sometimes, he sang a song about a frog he had invented. And once, he even drew a detective badge for the teddy bear to remember who saved him! Each day, he liked being an older brother more and more.

"Maybe one day I'll teach Lily how to solve riddles?" he wondered as he stacked the blocks.

"We're going to be the best team of detectives in the world!"

And who knows what adventures still awaited them? Jake and Lily's house suddenly became a place full of secrets to discover, and the teddy bear - well, the teddy bear never got lost for long because he had Jake, the best big brother in the world.

2. Super Siblings to the Rescue!

A long time ago, in a house where you could smell warm bread and that was full of colorful pictures on the walls, there lived a family that loved each other very much. There were Mom and Dad - always ready to hug or tell a fairy tale - and David, the older brother with a heart as big as the sun. David had hair sticking out in all directions and eyes sparkled when he had a new idea. For a few months, there was also Sarah at home - a little sister who could make everyone laugh with her cooing, but sometimes... Oh dear, how she could cry!

One day, the house became noisy. Very loud. Sarah had been crying since morning, softly, like a little kitten, and then louder, as if she wanted to sing a song but had forgotten the words. Her mother walked around the room with her in her arms, rocking her and humming a lullaby about a teddy bear that walks in the woods. Dad tried to calm her down by showing her funny faces - once, he was a frog, sometimes a clown, and once, he even pretended that his nose was a big balloon. But nothing worked. Sarah was still sobbing, and her face was as red as a tomato.

David was sitting in his room and drawing a rocket that was going to the moon. He heard his little sister crying and saw his mom and dad frowning more and more.

"Oh, poor Sarah," he thought. - "And poor parents too. They look like they've had enough."

He got up, threw his crayons on the desk, and decided to look into the living room.

"Mom, Dad, what's going on?" He asked, standing in the doorway.

Mom sighed and hugged Sarah tighter. "We don't know, David. Sarah cries and cries, and we have no idea how to calm her down. Maybe she's hungry? Maybe tired? Or perhaps something hurts her?

"We've tried everything," Dad added, making a tired lion face.

"I even danced like a duck, but that only made her angrier!"

David looked at his little sister. Her little hands waved in the air, and tears flowed like trickles. He felt that he wanted to help. "I'm an older brother, aren't I?" he thought.

"Superbrothers always save the day!" He came closer and asked:

"Can I try?"

Mom smiled weakly. "Sure, David. You are so lovely that you want to help.

Dad patted him on the shoulder. "You are our little hero. Do your best!"

David took a deep breath and began to think.

"What does Sarah like? What makes her smile?" First, he tried to pick up her favorite rattle - the one with colorful balls that rattle like rain on the roof. He shook her in front of her face, but Sarah just narrowed her eyes and cried even louder.

"Okay, that's not it," muttered David and put down the rattle.

Then he thought of the teddy bear, the one with one ear bigger than the other. He ran to Sarah's bed, grabbed the stuffed animal, and put it under his sister's nose.

"Look, Sarah, your friend is back!" - he chirped. Sarah looked at the teddy bear but then turned her head and began to sob again. David scratched his head.

"A difficult matter," he thought. - "But I won't give up!"

Mom and Dad looked at him with hope.

"David, you're so persistent," Mom said quietly.

"We can see that you care a lot."

"You're right," Dad added.

"You're the best big brother Sarah could ever have."

These words made David feel like a real superhero.

"I have to come up with something brilliant!" he decided.

He sat down on the carpet next to the couch where his mother rocked Sarah and began to think about what used to work. Suddenly, he remembered one thing: Sarah always calmed down when she heard something funny or strange.

"Or maybe..." - he thought and smiled broadly.

He got up, walked over to his little sister, and made the dumbest sounds he knew. First, he smacked as if he were kissing the air:

"Smack, smack, smack!".

Then he chuckled like a bit of chicken: " Cluck cluck!" In the end, he made a long, funny "Brrrrr" sound as if he were a car that slides on ice. Mom and Dad looked at him in surprise, but suddenly, something amazing happened—Sarah stopped crying!

Her little lips quivered, then stretched in a big smile. Instead of sobbing, she let out a soft, joyful squeal as if to say,

"Oh, I like it!" David didn't stop - now he pretended that his fingers were tiny spiders that tickled her tummy.

Sarah started laughing, and her laughter sounded like bells in the wind.

Mom and Dad opened their mouths in surprise. - David, you are a genius! Mother called and hugged him tightly. "How did you do it?"

"You're our superhero!" Dad added, lifting David up like a sack of potatoes. "You saved us all!"

David laughed and looked at Sarah, who was still giggling and waving her hands.

"It's simple," he said.

"Sarah likes it when it's fun. And I'm her big brother, so I have to make her laugh, right?

Mom nodded. "You're right, David. You are someone very important to her.

"And for us, too," Dad added.

"Thanks to you, the house is peaceful again."

From that day on, David became a specialist in calming Sarah. When she started whining, he would make funny sounds or make silly faces—once he was a frog, sometimes a huge balloon, and once he pretended that his nose was running out of his face. Sarah always laughed, and Mom and Dad looked at him with pride.

"You are our treasure," they said, and David felt as if he had an invisible super brother badge on his chest.

In the evenings, when Sarah fell asleep, David would sit by her bed and whisper:

"Don't worry, sister. I'll always make you laugh when you're sad."

And then he returned to his rockets and blocks, dreaming of more adventures in which he would save the day, not only for Sarah but for the whole family, because being an older brother is the best mission in the world!

3. Older Brother Badge

Once upon a time, in a house where there were drawings of children's hands on the walls and sunflowers taller than the fence in the garden, there lived a family full of joy. There were Mom and Dad - always ready to play and cook together - and Frank, a boy with freckles on his nose and a smile as wide as a river. Frank loved playing football and making up stories about dragons that flew above the clouds. For a few months, he also had a younger sister, Olivia - a little girl who cooed like a sparrow and loved to look at colorful things.

One Saturday morning, the house was cheerful and noisy. Mom was baking pancakes, and Dad was playing "Who can catch the ball faster?" with Frank in the backyard. Frank was running, laughing, and calling out every now and then:

"Dad, look what a high jump!".

Dad always answered: "Awesome, Frank, you are a master jumper!".

Then they returned home, where Olivia was waiting, sitting in her car seat with big eyes and a small rattle in her hand. My mother put a plate of pancakes on the table and said:

"Frank, can you help me feed Olivia?" You're so good at taking care of her.

Frank smiled. "Sure, Mom! "

He replied and handed his sister a piece of pancake crushed into mush. Olivia laughed, and a few drops landed on his T-shirt. Everyone laughed, and Dad patted him on the shoulder. - You're a super brother, Frank!

But after dinner, something changed. Neighbors came to the house - Mrs. Sophia with her son Max and Mr. Mark with his daughter Ava. They brought a small gift for Olivia - a beautiful, colorful carousel that was spinning over the cot. Everyone gathered around Olivia to see how she looked at the spinning animals.

"How sweet she is!" - said Mrs. Sophia.

"These ponds are like two small lakes! - added Mr. Mark.

Mom and Dad were smiling, and Frank was standing aside, holding his ball.

At first, Frank is happy that Olivia is liked by the guests. But after a while, he noticed that everyone was talking only about her - about how nicely she looked, how she waved her arms, how great she looked in the new merry-go-round. No one asked about his jumps in the yard or about the dragon he invented yesterday.

"Am I important too?" he thought, squeezing the ball tighter.

He felt like a balloon with air escaping - it was there, but no one noticed him.

Finally, he sat down on the couch and started bouncing the ball on the floor - bam, bam, bam. His mother looked at him and immediately approached. - Frank, what's going on? She asked gently, crouching next to him.

Frank shrugged. -I do not know... everyone looks at Olivia, and I... Well, maybe I'm not doing anything cool.

Mother stroked his head. "Oh, Frank, you do a lot of cool things!" You're the best big brother Olivia could have. Thanks to you, he laughs and feels safe. And for us, you are a real treasure.

-"Truly?" Frank asked, looking up.

"Really," replied Dad, who had just approached.

"Your jumps are amazing, and dragon stories are something only you can come up with. You are important to all of us."

Frank smiled shyly, but before he could say anything, a quiet sob came from Olivia's seat. The little girl started crying - at first quietly, and then louder and louder, waving her hands and wrinkling her nose. Mrs. Sophia approached the merry-go-round and turned it faster, and Mr. Mark tried to talk:

"Come on, now, little princess!".

But Olivia just shook her head and cried even more.

Frank looked at his sister and narrowed his eyes as if he were solving a riddle.

"I think there's too much going on here," he said out loud.

- "It's too loud, too many people, and Olivia is tired."

Mother raised her eyebrows. "You're right, Frank. You're so perceptive!

Dad nodded. "Maybe he really needs a moment of peace."

Frank thought for a moment and then said:

"You know what? I'll go outside the house to play football. Anyone want to play with me?"

Max, Sophia's son, jumped up with joy.

- "I want to! I like playing football!"

Ava, Mr. Mark's daughter, also clapped her hands. -"Me too! Will we play in teams?"

Dad smiled. "Okay, I'm going too. I can't miss such fun! "

Frank caught the ball, and a small group went out into the yard. Mom stayed inside with Olivia and Mrs. Sophia, who offered to sing a quiet lullaby to her. Outside, Frank began to toss the ball and invent the rules of the game:

"Whoever hits that tree gets a point!"

Max and Ava were running after him, laughing and trying to take the ball away from him, and Dad pretended to be a goalkeeper, making funny faces.

It became quieter inside the house. Olivia stopped crying, listening to the delicate voice of Mrs. Sophia. Her mother smiled at her and whispered,

"Frank was right. He really knows his little sister." After a while, Olivia fell asleep with her thumb in her mouth, and the merry-go-round was spinning slowly over her head. In the yard, Frank was running, jumping, and laughing until he was out of breath. "You're as fast as a dragon!" Winnie called, trying to catch up with him.

"And you're jumping like a kangaroo!" - added Ava, falling over on the grass with laughter.

Dad grabbed Frank in his arms and said,

"You're not only a jumping champion; you're a super brother. Thanks to you, Olivia calmed down, and we had the best fun in the world! "

When they got home, Mother waited with a smile. "Olivia is sleeping like an angel, and that's thanks to you, Frank.

You knew what she needed, and you gave us all a breather.
"

Frank looked at his sleeping sister and felt his heart grow.

"It's nice to be a brother," he said quietly.

That evening, Frank sat at the table, took out crayons, and drew a gold badge with the inscription "Super Brother." He showed it to his parents, and his dad said,

"You deserve it like no one else.

His mother added: "You are our treasure, Frank, and the best brother to Olivia. "

From that day on, Frank knew that being an older brother was something he could be proud of. Sometimes, he played ball tossing with Olivia; sometimes, he told her about dragons, and sometimes, he just took everyone to the yard to give her a moment of peace. His parents always praised him, and he felt like a hero, not only for Olivia but for the whole family. He knew that this badge shone brightest in his heart when he saw that everyone was happy because of him.

We'd love to hear your thoughts!

If you enjoyed this book, we would appreciate it if you could leave a review.

Your feedback means a lot and helps other readers discover our stories.

4. The Great Toddler Race

A long time ago, in a house surrounded by an orchard full of apple trees, where the wind rustled in the leaves, and there was always a bowl of fruit on the table, there lived a family that loved to play together. There was Mom and Dad - always willing to sing songs and make dumplings - and Stanley, a boy with red curls and a voice as loud as a bell. Stanley liked to set up tracks for his trains and race against the wind in the yard. For a few months, he also had a younger brother, Leo - a toddler who loved to wave his hands and squeal with joy as if the world was a big surprise.

One warm afternoon, cheerful sounds resounded in the house. Mom was cutting apples for apple pie, and Dad was playing a simple melody on the guitar, humming about a happy bear. Stanley was running around the room with the wooden train, shouting: "Clothes! The fastest train in the world!" Leo was lying on his tummy on a colorful blanket, supporting himself with his hands and looking at his brother with delight. He was a few months old and still couldn't fall over, but he was spinning around like a little worm, trying to catch his feet.

Mom glanced at Leo and smiled.

"Do you think he's going to do his first rollover today? That would be a big day!"

Dad put down his guitar and nodded.

"Who knows?"

Leo has a lot of energy; something is afoot.

Stanley stopped his train and ran to the blanket.

"If he falls, it's going to be like a race!" He cried, his curls jumping with excitement. - Leo vs. Stanley, who can do more!

Mother laughed. "Great idea, Stanley. You always come up with something funny! "

Stanley knelt next to Leo and began to cheer him on. "Come on, Leo, roll over!" You are the strongest! - he said, waving his hands like a fan at a match.

Leo looked at him, squealed happily, and waved his legs as if to say:

"Okay, brother, look at this!" Stanley clapped and shouted: "Leo, Leo, you can do it!"

And then something amazing happened. Leo tensed like a small spring, waved his hands, and then - hop! He rolled over from his tummy to his back. He was now lying on the blanket, his eyes blinking and smiling so broadly that he showed his two little teeth. Mom and Dad stood up from their seats.

- Bravo, Leo! Mom cried, raising her hands.

"You are a master of rollovers!" Dad added, clapping.

But Stanley had a bigger plan. - This is not the end! He said, running for his ball and the little train. - We will do a great toddler race!

Dad raised an eyebrow. -Race? Tell me!

Stanley smiled from ear to ear. "Leo will roll over, and I will ride the train and roll the ball. We'll see who can make more moves! "

Mom brought a small bell from the kitchen. "Okay, I'll be the judge." Ready? Start!

Stanley stood next to Leo with the ball in his hand. - "One, two, three - let's go! "

He shouted, and mom rang the bell. Leo started waving his legs again, trying to roll back over on his tummy. Stanley rolled the ball across the room, and then pushed the train, shouting:

"Clothes! One point for me!"

Leo did not lag behind. He wrinkled his nose, tensed up, and – hop! He rolled over on his tummy. Dad clapped.

– A point for Leo!

Stanley laughed. – "Great, brother! "

He said, quickly pushing the train once more, then tossed the ball up and caught it.

"Two for me!"

The race was in full swing. Leo rolled over once on his back, once on his tummy, and his every move caused shouts of joy. Stanley ran with the ball and the train, cheering on his brother:

"Leo, you are as fast as the wind! You go!".

Mom and Dad laughed as they watched their siblings turn an ordinary afternoon into a grand adventure. Finally, Leo got tired and laid his head on the blanket, cooing quietly, and Stanley sat down next to him, out of breath and happy.

"And who won?" Mom asked, raising the bell.

Stanley looked at Leo and smiled.

-" I think both of them! Leo fell three times, and I made five moves. But together we are the best! "

Dad hugged them both. "You're right, Stanley. You are an unbeatable team.

Mom nodded. "And this race was a brilliant idea. You're a superbrother, Stanley."

Stanley looked at Leo, who stretched out his hand to him, as if to say: "We had a great time, brother!". Pride sparkled in their eyes, and a wide smile lit up their face.

"It's good to have a brother," he said quietly.

"We can race and be in the same team."

That evening, Stanley sat at the table, took out crayons, and drew two medals - one for himself with the inscription "Master of Tracks" and the other for Leo with the inscription "Master of Revolutions." He hung them on the refrigerator door, and Dad said, "These are your trophies." Every little success of Leo is also your success, Stanley.

"Because we're a team," added Stanley, and Leo gurgled as if he agreed.

From that day on, Stanley celebrated Leo's every step - when he caught the ball for the first time, when he sat down or when he started crawling. Each time he organized a small "race" - sometimes with a train, sometimes with a ball, and sometimes he just ran around it, shouting:

"Leo, you're great!".

With each passing day, he felt that their bond was getting stronger, and playing together made them the best siblings in the area.

In the evenings, when Leo fell asleep, Stanley would sit by his bed and whisper:

"You are my favorite player, little brother."

And then he would go back to his trains, dreaming of new races in which they always won together.

Part 2: Learning to Share the Spotlight

5. Mysterious Treasure Hunt

A long time ago, in a house where old balls lay under the stairs and pots with cacti stood on the windowsill, there lived a family that loved to solve puzzles. There was Mom and Dad - always ready to play guessing games or fry pancakes with jam - and Tony, a boy with disheveled hair and pockets full of interesting trinkets. Tony liked to collect bottle caps, build towers from them, and invent roles for them - some were guards, others treasure caches. What he loved most in the world was his little metal toy car with red wheels—shiny, fast, with his dad's birthday signature on the bottom. For a few months, he also had a younger brother, Chris, a toddler who loved to grab everything that moved and laugh like a little drum until everyone around him smiled.

One cloudy afternoon, Tony was sitting in his room, arranging a new tower of nuts. This time, it was to be an impregnable fortress with high walls and a place for the king - his red car. He reached for the shelf where he usually kept it, but... The shelf was empty! Tony frowned and started searching. He knocked over a box of toys - only blocks and old balls. He looked under the carpet - only dust and a lost pencil. He even checked behind the bed, where he found a striped sock but no sign of the car.

"That's impossible! - muttered. "My treasure couldn't just disappear!"

He ran down the stairs to the living room, stomping like a little elephant. Mom was arranging blocks with Chris on the carpet, and Dad was reading the newspaper on the couch and drinking tea. Chris sat in his armchair, waving a large, yellow spoon as if he were conducting an invisible orchestra.

- Mom, Dad, my toy car is gone! Tony shouted, standing in front of them with his hands on his hips.

- Surely Chris took him! He always grabs my stuff as soon as he sees it!

My mother looked up from the blocks and smiled. - Tony, Chris doesn't walk yet. How could he take something from your bookshelf?

"Well, but he has fast hands!" Tony insisted. "Yesterday, he grabbed my pencil, and the day before yesterday, he pulled himself up to the table and threw my nut off. !He must have done something with it!!"

Dad put down the newspaper and laughed.

- Detective Tony, maybe instead of looking for the guilty one, you should look for them together? You are a master at finding things, and Chris can be your helper.

Tony wrinkled his nose as if he was smelling something suspicious, but then his eyes lit up.

"Okay, let's do a Mystery Treasure Hunt!" He said, clapping his hands.

"Chris will be on my team, even if he loses my toy car. We will find it, and it will be something extra!!"

Mom nodded. "Great idea. You're a super brother, Tony.

Dad lifted Chris from the car seat and said: "Let's go, crew!" Captain Tony is driving!

Tony ran to get a piece of paper and a pencil and then sat down on the carpet, drawing a map of the house. He did it on a grand scale - he called the living room "Land of Blocks" and drew a tower of blocks there, the kitchen became a "Bay of Spoons" with a large pot, and his room was named "Tower of Nuts" with a high wall. At the bottom of the map, he wrote in large letters: "X - here is the treasure!". He handed Chris a yellow spoon and said,

"It's your compass, little brother." Show me the way, and I'll seek. Ready?

Chris squeezed the spoon happily and waved it in the air as if he really knew where to go.

The first stop was "Blockland". Tony dived under the couch, pulling out an old ball and a crumpled piece of paper, but he didn't find the car.

"There's nothing here!" - cried.

Dad picked up Chris to "direct" the spoon. Chris pointed to the coffee table, so Tony looked underneath. All he found there were his dad's newspapers and cookie crumbs.

"Hmmm, it's a difficult matter," muttered Tony, shaking his hands.

"But pirates, never give up!" Chris, keep pointing!

They set off to the "Bay of Spoons". Mom opened the drawers with spoons and forks, and Tony looked into the basket with Chris's toys, which were standing in the corner of the kitchen. He pulled out a rubber duck, a stuffed dog, and a plastic cup, but there was no sign of the red car.

"Maybe he threw it into the pot?" - he wondered aloud. He even checked the big soup pot but found only leftover pasta. Chris laughed as if to say: "Search better, brother!".

Tony looked at him and said:

"You little cunning, you're having fun, aren't you?"

Finally, they returned to the "Nut Tower". Tony knocked over the box with the caps until they scattered on the floor like colorful rain. He looked under the pillow - nothing. He searched the trash can - only candy wrappers.
"Where are you, my king of the tower?"
He muttered, sitting down on the carpet. Chris, still in his dad's arms, waved his spoon and squealed, pointing to the corner of the room. Tony looked in that direction and noticed something shiny under the cabinet.
"Wait, what's that?"

He said, approaching on all fours. He reached out and... He pulled out his toy car! The red circles glistened in the lamplight.

"I've got him!" He cried triumphantly, jumping up. "But how did he get there?"

Mom smiled. "Maybe you knocked him over yesterday when you were building the tower, and he rolled under the cabinet?"

Tony laughed, shaking his head. - I think so. It wasn't Chris, it was me who lost him!

But the search is not over yet. When Tony got up, Chris squealed louder and pointed to the corner with his spoon again. Tony looked more carefully and noticed something else - a small, shiny coin that was lying next to the place where the car was. He picked it up and showed it to his parents. "Look, a real treasure!" It's pirate gold!

Dad clapped his hands.

- Come on, Chris found something better than your toy car!

Mom hugged them both. "You are a great team. Together, you find things that no one would have thought of.

Tony looked at Chris, who stretched out his hand to him as if to say:

"We had a great time, brother!".

"Thanks, Chris," he said with a smile.

"You are my best helper. I thought you lost my treasure, and you helped me find two!"

A wave of pride washed over them, leaving a spark of joy in their heart.

"It's nice to have a brother," he added quietly. "Even if he is not crawling, he is still in my crew.

That evening, Tony sat at the table with a piece of paper and crayons. He drew a new map - a more detailed one, with the "Bottle Nut Tower" entwined with snakes (i.e., curtain strings) and an "X" in the corner of the room where they found the treasure. At the bottom, he wrote: "Tony and Chris - the Best Searchers." He hung the map above the bed and told Christopher, who grumbled in response,

"This is our first trip together, little brother. We will search for treasures the world has never seen before!"

From that day on, Tony and Chris often organized searches. Sometimes, they looked for lost nuts under the sofa, sometimes shiny pebbles in the garden, and once, they even found their mother's old hairpin in a crack in the floor. Tony always gave Chris a "compass" - sometimes a spoon, sometimes a rattle - and shouted:

"Point, helper!".

Chris squealed and waved, and Tony searched, laughing when they found something. Their parents looked at them with pride, and their dad once said: "You are like real pirates - one is in charge, the other is guarding the treasure."

In the evenings, when Chris fell asleep, Tony would sit by his bed and whisper:

"You're in my team, little pirate."

Together, we will find all the treasures of the world. "And then he went back to his caps, building new towers, in which there was always room for him and Chris" - the best crew in the world.

6: Sharing Is Hard (But Not Impossible!)

Matt was speeding his blue car along a track made of books and boxes that he had built in the middle of the living room.

"Warum! The fastest car in the world! "

He shouted, his voice bouncing off the walls. The track was perfect: an atlas ramp, a cardboard tunnel, and a long, straight road to the finish. Matt had a plan in his head - to organize a great race and beat his record. But suddenly, something disrupted his championship competition.

His younger brother, John, who had been sitting on the couch with their mother, climbed down on the carpet and grabbed the blue car in his little hands. "Gu-gu!" He called, waving it in the air like a trophy. Saliva dripped from his mouth, and his eyes sparkled with joy.

- Hey, John, give it back! Matt shouted, running up to his brother. "It's my best car, you can't take it!"

Mom put down the book she was reading and looked at Matt.

"Matt, he just wants to play. Why don't you let him hold it for a while?"

"But it's mine!" Matt insisted, stamping his foot.

"I always want my stuff, and I have nothing for myself!"

Dad came out of the kitchen, carrying a plate of sliced apples.

"What's going on here, guys?" He asked, sitting down in the armchair.

- Matt, I know you like your car, but John is small and wants to be like you. Maybe you will find a way to share?"

Matt crossed his arms and looked at John, who was now drooling over the blue car as if it were a lollipop. "And what if he spoils it? Or if he loses it? I don't want to share if he takes everything!" He grumbled.

For a moment, Matt stood with a grumpy face, watching John playing with his treasure. He felt as if someone had stolen a piece of his track - and the best one! But then he noticed something interesting. John not only held the car but also tried to push it on the carpet, just like Matt had done before. "Hmmm..." he muttered under his breath.

"Maybe he wants to race like me?"

He ran to the toy box in the corner of the living room and started rummaging inside. He pulled out an old, green car - a little scratched, with one wheel that swayed.

"Okay, John, I have a plan!" - cried.

Mom raised an eyebrow. "What's the plan, Matt?"

- Fair distribution! He said with a smile. He approached John, gently took the blue car out of his hands, and handed him the green one.

"It's yours, and the blue one is mine. But we're going to have fun together, okay?"

John squeezed happily, clutching the green car, and Matt breathed a sigh of relief, holding his treasure. Dad clapped his hands.

- Come on, Matt, you are like a master of justice!

Matt returned to his track and started to redo it. He made two tracks next to each other - one for himself, with high ramps made of books and a tunnel made of cardboard, and the other simpler, for John, with pillows as hills and a puzzle board as a bridge. - It will be the Great Brothers' Race! -Told.

He put his blue car at the start and sat John next to his track with a green car in his hands.

- One, two, three - go! He shouted, pushing his car. John, imitating his brother, pushed his car on the pillow. The green car fell on its side, and John laughed so loudly that he jumped.

Matt looked at him and laughed, too.

"Okay, your car likes rolling, and mine likes speed. It's fair! -Said.

He pushed his car through the tunnel, doing a "warm!" and John rolled his car on the pillow, sometimes throwing it on the carpet.

"You're a master of chaos, John!" - Matt shouted, correcting the track after another "accident" of his brother.

Mom and Dad looked at them with a smile.

"Matt, it's a brilliant way to share," said my mother. "Everyone has something on their own, and you have fun together.

"You're a super brother," Dad added, cutting the apple into smaller pieces.

- You made John feel part of the race.

Matt did not stop playing.

- Wait, that's not all! He said, running to get more toys. He pulled out of the box an old, plastic plane with one wing and a small truck without wheels. "John, this is your fleet!" He called, placing them on his brother's track.

"You have your machines, I have mine, but we're racing together!"

John squealed with joy, grabbing the plane and pushing it on the pillow. The truck slid off the "bridge" and landed on Matt's track, overturning the blue car.

"Oh no, an air attack!"

Matt laughed, pretending that his car was crashing. John clapped his hands as if it was the best moment of the day.

Throughout the afternoon, the brothers held their races. Matt whizzed the blue car through tunnels and ramps, making engine noises, and John rolled his toys, sometimes throwing them toward his brother. Once, John's truck landed straight in Matt's cardboard tunnel, blocking the road. - John, you little saboteur! Matt shouted, pulling her out and pretending to run away from the "enemy." Mom and Dad were laughing as they watched the carpet turn into a playground full of chaos and joy.

When the sun began to set, mom suggested a break. "Why don't we eat an apple pie and take a break from racing?" She said, putting the plate on the table. Matt sat down next to John and handed him a small piece of apple.

"You're in my team, little brother," he said.

"We share tracks, toys, and even apple pie!

John was groaning as if he wanted to say:

"Okay, brother!".

A proud smile crept across his face, impossible to hide.

"You know what?" He muttered to himself.

- Sharing is not so difficult when you divide well.

That evening, Matt drew a sign for his team - two cars, blue and green, speeding side by side. He hung it over the toy box and said to John:

"This is our logo, brother. We are a racing team!"

John waved his hand as if saluting and his parents smiled proudly.

"Matt, you are a master of sharing," said dad.

"You made it fun for both of you."

From that day on, Matt came up with new ways to have fun together. Sometimes, he built John a small track out of blocks; sometimes, he gave him old toys for the "fleet," and sometimes, he let him push the blue car - but only once! With each passing day, he felt that sharing could be fun, especially when John laughed and clapped as if Matt was his hero.

"You're in my crew, little driver," he sometimes whispered to him before bedtime. And then he would fall asleep, dreaming of new races where there was always room for both of them.

7: The Baby Translator

On a rainy afternoon, Tony ran into the living room like a storm with wet shoes, leaving muddy marks on the floor.

- Mom, Dad! I found the biggest puddle in history!

He shouted, waving his arms as if he were talking about the capture of pirate treasure. His dark hair stuck to his forehead, and in his jacket pocket, there was water splashing, which he had poured from a puddle "for later." Before his mother could say: "Tony, shoes!" he heard a familiar sound

- "Gu-gu-ga!" - coming from the corner of the room. It was his little brother, Frank, who sat in a car seat and waved his hands like a small windmill.

Tony stopped in mid-step and looked at his brother. Frank was wearing a funny hat with a pom-pom on it, which slipped over his eyes, and a rubber key in his mouth, drooling it like a lollipop.

"What are you talking about again, Frank?"

Tony asked, taking off his jacket and throwing it on the couch. Mom, who had just come in from the kitchen with a towel, sighed.

- Tony doesn't speak; he just guga. But maybe he wants you to play with him?

Dad, sitting at the table with a cup of tea, laughed. "Or he speaks his language, and you, Tony, have to translate it!"

Tony narrowed his eyes as if he was solving a riddle. - Translate? -Muttered.

"Okay, Frank, what are you fuming?"

He walked over to the car seat and crouched down, looking his brother straight in the eye. Frank squealed: "Ba-ba-gu!" and waved the key. Tony raised an eyebrow and then smiled broadly.

-Yes! He says: "Tony, give me the biggest piece of apple pie because I'm hungry like a dragon!"

My mother lifted her head from the towel. "Apple pie?" Frank doesn't eat cake yet!

- But that's how I heard it! Tony replied, getting up and running to the kitchen. He returned with a plate on which lay a small piece of apple.

"Okay, dragon, this is for you," he said, handing it to Frank. The toddler grabbed the apple and began to drool over it, cooing with joy.

Dad put down the cup and clapped his hands.

- Tony, you are a translator of children's gugs! What else does Frank say?

Tony sat down on the carpet next to the car seat and pricked up his ears. Frank let out a long "Guuuu-da-da!" and pointed with the key to the window, behind which the rain was drumming against the windows. Tony scratched his head and then jumped to his feet.

- Okay, now he says: "Tony, go outside and bring me the biggest puddle, I want to splash in it!"

Mom laughed. - Tony can't splash in a puddle!

- But I can! - said Tony with a twinkle in his eye.

"I'll translate it in my own way. "

He ran to the hallway, grabbed a plastic cup and ran out into the yard. He came back after a minute, wet as a duck, with a cup full of rainwater.

"Please, Frank, your puddle!" He called, placing his cup in front of the seat. Frank dipped his hand into it, splashing water on the carpet, and squealed with delight.

The parents looked at Tony with a mixture of surprise and amusement.

"You're good, Tony," said dad.

"You have a talent for understanding Frank.

- It's easy when you listen! Tony replied, wiping his wet hands on his pants.

"He's a fool, and I know what he means. He pricked up his ears again, because Frank gave another "Ma-ma-gu-gu!" and stretched his hands towards the couch. Tony looked at his mother, then at the couch, and suddenly clapped his hands.

-Yes!

Frank says: "Tony, build me a big mountain of pillows, I want to be the king of the castle!"

My mother raised an eyebrow. "The king of the castle?"

"Of course! - Tony called and rushed into action. He grabbed all the cushions from the couch, threw them on the carpet, and began to lay the high tower. Dad picked Frank up from the car seat and sat him on top, and Tony climbed next to him, pretending to be a guard.

"King Frank, your castle is ready!" He said, saluting. Frank snorted loudly as if giving orders and then dropped the pillow to the floor, laughing until he cried.

Throughout the afternoon, Tony was running around the house, "explaining" Frank's guganing to various requests. When Frank said, "Da-da-ba!" and pointed to his dad, Tony announced:

"He wants dad to sing a song about pirates!"

Dad grabbed a newspaper, rolled it up into a trumpet and sang in a deep voice:

'Hey ho, I'm going to the sea!' Frank clapped his hands, and Tony pretended to row in an invisible boat. Then Frank said, "Gu-gu-di!" and looked at the lamp. -Yes! He wants us to do a light show!

Tony cried. He pulled a flashlight out of the drawer, turned it on, and began to shine on the ceiling, creating dancing patches of light.

Frank squealed with joy, trying to catch the rays with his hands.

My mother looked at it all with a smile.

"Tony, you're like a detective of children's gugs," she said, bringing a plate of cookies from the kitchen. "How do you know what Frank wants?"

Tony shrugged, taking the cookie. "I listen and guess. He grumbles, and I figure out what it could mean. It's like playing pirate codes! He pricked up his ear again, because Frank gave a quiet "Ba-gu-gu..." and yawned.

Tony smiled. - Oh, now he says: "Tony, take me on a great adventure to the land of dreams!"

Dad laughed. "I guess it's time for a nap, huh?"

"But my style!" - said Tony. He grabbed a blanket, laid it on the floor like a raft, and put a pillow on it.

- Frank, get on the ship of dreams! -Cried.

Mom picked up Frank and put him on the "raft", and Tony began to pretend that he was paddling, humming softly: "Szzz... szzzz... we are sailing through a sea of clouds!".

From that day on, Tony became a master of Frank's translation - and a super brother to the fullest.

8: The Super Secret Big Brother Club

Saturday afternoon was quite ordinary. Philip was sitting on the carpet in the living room, focused on building a fortress out of blocks. It was huge - it had a high tower, secret passages, and even a place for a catapult (i.e., a rubber ball that could be launched into the air). Right next to him, in his car seat, sat his younger brother Alex. He was still tiny, and instead of helping with the construction, he held a rubber block in his hand and drooled it intensely as if it was the best dessert in the world.

Then Dad entered the living room. He held an old wooden box in his hands and had a mysterious smile on his face - that smile that Philip knew very well. It was the smile of a grand plan.

"Philip," Dad said, sitting down on the floor,

"The big day has come. The day you will move to the next level of elderhood."

Philip looked at him suspiciously.

"A higher level?" What does that mean?

Dad put the box between them and lightly struck the lid.

"This means you have the chance to join the extremely secret, super-important, and absolutely amazing Secret Club of the Superbrothers.

Philip straightened up immediately. Secret club?! That was something!

- What do you have to do to join it? He asked, narrowing his eyes.

Dad carefully opened the box. Inside there were things that looked like treasures: an old flashlight, a notebook with a cover with drawings of lightning, a wooden badge engraved with the letters "TSB" and... cape?

Philip raised his eyebrows.

"Do you need a cape for this club?"

Dad nodded solemnly.

-Of course. After all, the older brother is a bit like a superhero. And every superhero has his cape.

Philip smiled broadly. He loved superheroes! If being an older brother meant superpowers, then he was ready.

Dad cleared his throat and lifted three fingers.

"But to become a member of the club, you must know and follow the three rules of the Super Brothers.

Philip nodded.

"Come on, dad." I'm ready.

Dad pointed to Alex, who was trying to push the block into his mouth, and looked at Philip meaningfully.

- Rule one: Superbrother always comes up with the best games. It could be building castles out of pillows, rescue missions for lost teddy bears, or racing on all fours around the living room.

Philip looked at Alex, who was now staring intently at his foot as if he had just discovered something amazing.

"Okay, that sounds easy. What's next?

Dad lifted the other finger.

- Rule two: Superbrother is always a protector. He must protect his little brother from monsters under the bed, a terrifying vacuum cleaner, and...

Dad leaned over and whispered:

- ... very green vegetables.

Philip chuckled.

"Alex defends himself against vegetables. Yesterday, his mother gave him peas, and he spit them straight on the floor.

Dad nodded appreciatively.

"Good reflexes. But coming back."

He lifted his third finger. - Rule three: The Secret Club of Superbrothers never reveals their secrets... especially to Mom!

Philip's eyes widened.

- Even to my mom?!

"Even your mom," Dad confirmed, making a serious face.

"Club affairs are our special mission."

Philip felt his excitement grow. Secret club, secrets, missions! It was the best thing that could have happened to him.

Dad reached into the box and pulled out a wooden badge.

"Do you accept the challenge?"

Philip shook the outstretched hand.

- I accept!

Dad pinned the badge to his shirt and then threw a cape over him.

"Welcome to the Secret Club of Superbrothers!"

Philip felt as if he had indeed become a hero. He stood up proudly and looked around the room.

"Okay, so where do we start?"

At that moment, Alex let out a joyful "Ba-ba-da!" and looked at the kitchen, smacking his lips.

Philip thought for a moment, then smiled broadly.

- Alex says: "Philip, bring me the biggest piece of cake because I'm hungry like a dragon!".

Dad raised his eyebrow.

-Seriously?

Philip nodded seriously.

- I have a super-brotherly intuition.

Dad sighed and shook his head in amusement.

- Okay, but before the cake mission... There is also the Diaper Mission.

Philip immediately sprang to his feet.

- The Superbrothers Club announces a break for more important tasks!

And he ran out of the room, followed by the sound of dad's laughter and Alex's joyful guggling.

That day, Philip understood one thing: being an older brother is not only a duty... It's a great adventure.

TSB

Part 3: The Fun (and Funny) Side of Sibling Life

9: A Baby on the Loose!

Tim was sitting in the yard, surrounded by his treasures - sticks that pretended to be swords and stones that were "dragon eggs." The sun was shining high, and he was finishing building a fortress of sand when he heard a strange sound—something like shuffling and giggling. He turned and saw his little brother, Alex, crawling through the grass at the speed of a small tank, leaving a trail of leaves and dirt behind him. - Alex, where did you come from?! Tim shouted, jumping to his feet. His brown hair jumped and a red light went off in his head:

"Alex is running away!"

Alex was eight months old and had recently discovered that crawling was the best fun in the world. A moment ago he was sitting with his mother on a blanket under an apple tree, playing with a wooden block, and now he was rushing towards the fence, guggling like a small engine: "Ga-ga-ga!". Tim threw down his "sword" and ran after him.

- Mom, Alex broke off!

He shouted, but Mom had just come into the house to get some juice, and Dad was mowing the grass at the other end of the garden, drowned out by the whirr of the lawnmower.

"Stop, little fugitive!" - Tim shouted, running across the lawn. Alex was as fast as a squirrel - his hands and knees were whizzing across the grass, and there was a wide smile on his face as if he knew he was doing something crazy. Tim dived to catch him, but Alex turned to the side and moved towards the chicken coop, where the hens were clucking as if they were cheering for the toddler.

"Oh no, you won't get in there!" - said Tim, accelerating. In his head, he already had the image of Alex covered with a chicken feather and the laughter of his mother, who would surely photograph it.

But before he reached the chicken coop, Alex changed direction again - this time he rushed to a large puddle left after yesterday's rain.

- Alex, not into the water! Tim shouted, imagining his brother all in the mud. He decided to act cleverly. "Okay, kid, we're going to make a game out of this!" - cried. "It's the Great Hunt for the Fleeing Treasure!"

Alex stumbled, as if he understood, and sped up, and Tim grabbed a stick from the ground, pretending it was a lasso. "I'm catching you, darling!" He said, swinging as if he were throwing an invisible rope. Alex laughed and turned towards the swing, leaving a trail of grass on his knees behind him.

Tim came up with another idea.

"Wait, we're changing the rules!" - shouted.

"You're a fast rabbit and I'm a rabbit hunter!"

He started jumping like a kangaroo, making big hops, and Alex stopped for a moment, looking at his brother with delight.

- Hop, hop, I'll catch you! - Tim shouted, jumping closer and closer.

Alex squealed and moved on, but now he was laughing so loudly that he slowed down, giving Tim a chance.

"Oh, now I have you!" - said Tim, running in a zigzag like a fox. Alex reached the swing and grabbed onto it's string, trying to pull himself up. Tim reached him just in time, grabbing him by the armpits and lifting him up.

"I caught the escaping treasure!" - he shouted triumphantly, and Alex waved his legs in the air, gumming:

"Ba-da-ga!" as if he wanted to say:

"That was great fun!"

Then mom came out from behind the house, carrying a jug of juice.

"What's going on here?" - she asked, seeing Tim with Alex in her arms and mud on their knees.

- Alex ran away, mom! - said Tim, putting his brother on the grass.

"But we made a game out of it - The Great Hunt for Escaping Treasure!"

Dad turned off the lawnmower and walked over, laughing.

- It seems that Alex is a fast player. How did you catch him, Tim?

"I was a rabbit hunter!" - replied Tim, showing his "lasso" made of a stick.

"I jumped, ran and pretended to catch him. He laughed and slowed down, so I won!"

Mum knelt next to Alex and wiped his hands with a handkerchief.

- Tim, you are brilliant. You have turned escape into fun.

"You're a superbrother," Dad added, patting him on the shoulder.

"Alex is growing like a weed, and you keep up with him like a real champion."

Tim looked at Alex, who was now sitting on the grass and playing with a stick that the "rabbit hunter" had left behind.

"You know what? He said quietly.

"It's nice to have a brother who moves so quickly. You have to chase him and laugh!

- He ran for his "sword" from the fortress and returned to Alex.

"Okay, little one, now you're a dragon and I'm a knight!" Run away and I'll catch you!

Alex squealed and moved on all fours towards the apple tree, and Tim ran after him, pretending to swing an invisible sword. "The dragon is fleeing!" Knight Tim on the trail! - he shouted, taking great strides.

For the rest of the afternoon, Tim and Alex played chases. Once Alex was a "fast turtle" and Tim was a tracker who pretended to look for tracks in the grass. Another time, Alex became a "pirate on a raft" (read: a blanket), and Tim became a captain who chased him with a "lasso" made of string. Mom brought juice and apples, and dad sat on a bench, taking pictures of their crazy play.

"Alex is growing like a rocket," said dad.

"And you, Tim, are his best guide."

When Alex finally got tired and sat down on the blanket, Tim knelt next to him.

"You're quick, little brother," he said, handing him a piece of apple.

"But I'll always catch you, because it's the best game in the world."

Alex was fumbling as if he wanted to say:

"We're chasing each other again!", and Tim laughed. "Okay, but first rest, the dragon got tired!"

That evening, Tim drew a map of the yard with Alex's escape route - from the blanket, through the puddle, to the swing. He called it the "Trail of the Fleeing Treasure" and hung it over his bed.

"This is our adventure, Alex," he said, looking at his sleeping brother in the crib.

"You're growing like a madman, and I'll run after you, because it's more fun than building fortresses."

From that day on, Tim turned every escape of Alex into a new game. When Alex crawled to the kitchen, he was a "cookie thief" and Tim was a "pantry keeper". When he rushed to the garden, he became a "mud monster" and Tim a "monster hunter". His parents laughed as they watched Tim chasing his brother, making faces and inventing new rules. "You're in my team, little fugitive," he sometimes whispered to him before bedtime. And then he would fall asleep, dreaming of more chases, in which their fun together would always win.

10: No More Yucky Kisses!

Nathan was sitting on the carpet in the living room, surrounded by his beloved dinosaur figurines. Triceratops was getting ready to attack Tyrannosaurus Rex when suddenly something wet dripped onto his hand.

-What is it?! He shouted, looking up.

Above him stood his little brother, Bob, with his mouth wet with saliva and his hands stretched out like those of a small zombie. Before Nathan could escape, Bob pounced on him, leaving a big, slippery kiss on his cheek. "Gu-gu-ba!" Bob cried, laughing as if it were the best joke in the world.

- Yuck, Bob, those wet kisses again!

Nathan groaned, wiping his face with the sleeve of his sweatshirt.

"It's disgusting!"

He got up and jumped back on the couch as if he were running away from the lava. Bob, undeterred, crawled behind him, dragging a teddy bear behind him and leaving a trail of saliva on the floor. Nathan looked at him with a face, as if he saw something really nasty.

"Mom, Dad, do something about this kissing monster!" - cried.

Mom walked into the living room with a laundry basket in her hands.

"Nathan, Bob just wants to show you that he likes you," she said with a smile, putting the basket on the table.

"But it's wet and smells of milk!" Nathan protested, hiding behind his pillow.

- I don't want any more yucky kisses!

Dad, who was reading a book in an armchair, raised his head.

"You know, Nathan, that's how little children show love. Maybe you'll find a way to like it?"

-Never! Nathan grumbled, grimacing. "It's like a dog licking, only worse!"

Bob did not give up. He pulled himself up on the couch, climbing onto the pillow, and threw himself at Nathan again, trying to leave another kiss. "Ba-da-ga!" He blurted, his wet face landing on his brother's forehead. Nathan squealed and jumped off the couch, running to his room. -No more! He shouted, slamming the door. He sat up on the bed, still wiping his face, and looked at his dinosaurs.

"A Tyrannosaurus has never had to put up with such things," he muttered.

But the peace did not last long. After a while, he heard shuffling and a quiet "gu-gu" at the door. Bob has reached his hideout! Nathan sighed and opened the door, and the little brother scrambled inside, pulling the teddy bear and smiling from ear to ear. "Why do you always follow me?" - asked Nathan, but Bob looked at him with his big eyes and blurted: "Ba-gu!" as if to say: "Because I like you, brother!". Nathan rolled his eyes and sat back on the bed. "Okay, but no more kisses, okay?" He said, pointing at his brother. Bob laughed and rushed forward, trying to grab Nathan by the leg.

"Oh no, again!" Nathan shouted, jumping down to the floor.

"I have to figure something out before you turn me into a slippery dinosaur!"

He took a deep breath and looked at his figurines. "Wait, maybe..." he muttered, and a light bulb lit up in his head.

"We'll make fun of it!" He ran to the locker, pulled out his mother's old headscarf and tied it around his head like a pirate bandana.

"I'm Captain Nathan, and you, Bob, are a wet sea monster!" He cried, grabbing a plastic sword from the toy box. Bob squealed with joy and set off on all fours, chasing his brother around the room.

Nathan jumped on the bed, pretending to avoid "sea attacks".

- Ha! You can't catch me, monster! He cried, swinging his sword.

Bob reached the bed and grabbed onto the edge, trying to climb up. When he finally climbed upstairs, he lunged at Nathan with another wet kiss - this time right in the nose!

"Yuck, a critical hit!" Nathan laughed, rolling over on his back. Bob sat on it, cooing and clapping his hands as if announcing victory.

Mom looked into the room when she heard a noise. "What are you doing here?" She asked, leaning against the doorframe.

"I'm fighting a wet sea monster!" - replied Nathan, pretending to push him away with his sword. "But he still wins with his kisses!"

Mom laughed. - It seems that Bob really wants to "defeat" you with love.

"Wet love," Nathan muttered, wiping his nose, but this time he smiled.

Dad came in behind Mom, holding a book.

"Maybe instead of fighting, you will accept his kisses as a badge of honor?"

He suggested, raising an eyebrow.

"After all, he is your faithful sailor."

Nathan looked at Bob, who was now playing with his sword, drooling his hand. "Badge, you say?" -Muttered. "Okay, so be it!" He stood up, adjusted his bandana, and said,

"Bob, you're my number one sea monster. But we have to set the rules - one kiss a day, the rest is a high five, okay?"

Bob blurted: "Da-ga!" and stretched out his hand, as if he wanted to give a high five. Nathan grabbed his tiny hand and shook it. - The deal is there! He said, and then picked up his brother and sat him down on the bed next to the dinosaurs.

For the rest of the afternoon, Nathan played with Bob, turning kisses into part of the game.

"Okay, Bob, now you're a dragon that breathes wet fire!"

He called, positioning the Triceratops as a shield. Bob threw himself at the figurine, leaving a trail of saliva on it, and Nathan pretended that the dragon had scored a point. "One-zero for you, dragon!" He laughed, wiping the dinosaur with his sleeve. Then they changed roles - Nathan was a knight, and Bob was the "king of the wet fortress", who threw kisses like magic missiles. Once Bob hit Nathan straight in the ear, and Nathan fell on the carpet, pretending to fall from the "spell".

"Oh no, a wet attack!" Rescue! - he cried, and Bob squealed with joy.

When the sun began to set, Mom called them for dinner. Nathan sat down at the table, and Bob was in his chair next to him.

"Nathan, how did the fight with the monster go?" Dad asked, slicing the bread.

"We drew," Nathan replied, impaling a potato on his fork. "But you know what?" His kisses are not as bad as they are made into a game.

Mom smiled. "So they're not yucks anymore?"

Nathan shrugged. "There are some, but Bob shows that he likes me. It's like his way of saying "you're cool, bro". So let him kiss - but only once a day!

Bob blurted: "Gu-ba!" and stretched out his hand with a crumb of bread, as if he wanted to share it. Nathan took the crumb and said:

"Thanks, little one. You're cool too."

That night, Nathan drew a badge - a golden star with the inscription "Hero of Wet Kisses". He hung it over the bed and looked at the sleeping Bob in the cot. "You're strange, little brother, but I like you," he whispered.

"Even with those wet kisses. "

Everything around him seemed brighter because they felt proud inside. Nathan understood that Bob's love was a little slippery and strange, but it was his way of saying "you're my brother", and that's better than a dry handshake.

From that day on, Nathan stopped running away from Bob's kisses. Sometimes he would turn his cheek and say,

"Okay, dragon, one shot!" - and Richie kissed him with a smile. Other times, he turned it into a game - he counted "hits" and pretended to fall from the excess of "power of love". His parents laughed when they saw Nathan accept the wet signs of his brother's feelings.

"You're in my crew, little monster," he whispered to him before bedtime. And then he'd fall asleep knowing that even the most yucky things can be cool if they mean someone loves you.

Family
Fun

11: The Sneaky Baby Ninja

Max was pretty sure his baby sister, Sophie, was not an ordinary baby. She might look small and helpless, but Max had seen things—things that made him believe she had secret ninja powers.

It all started one evening when Max was carefully building a towering castle out of blocks. He had spent nearly an hour making sure each block was perfectly balanced. Just as he placed the final piece, he turned around to grab his superhero figure to guard the castle.

That's when it happened. CRASH!

Max spun around. The castle was gone, and in its place sat Sophie, staring at him with wide, innocent eyes, her tiny hand resting on a fallen block.

"But… but you were all the way over there in your baby bouncer!" Max pointed in disbelief. He had only looked away for two seconds! How had she got across the room so fast?

Sophie blinked. Then she giggled.

Max narrowed his eyes. This wasn't an accident. This was the work of a Sneaky Baby Ninja.

The following day, Max decided to investigate. He set up a test, placing his favorite stuffed dragon, Sir Fluffington, on the coffee table. If Sophie indeed had ninja skills, she would strike when no one was looking.

Max pretended to read a book but kept one eye on Sophie, who was lying on her play mat, waving her tiny feet in the air.

Minutes passed. Nothing happened. Maybe he had imagined it?

Then—whoosh!—Sophie was on the move in a blink. She rolled, scooted, and somehow, without making a sound, grabbed Sir Fluffington!

Max gasped. "Aha! I knew it! You are a ninja, Sophie!"

Sophie clutched the stuffed dragon, looking completely pleased with herself.

Max grinned. If his baby sister was a ninja, then he had a new mission: to train her. Every great ninja needed a master, after all. And who better than her big brother?

From that day on, Max became Sophie's official ninja teacher. He taught her the art of stealth (hiding behind pillows), the skill of surprise (jumping out with giggles), and the power of speed (crawling races down the hallway).

But Sophie had some tricks of her own. She mastered the Silent Grab, where she could snatch

anything Max left unguarded. She perfected the Sudden Distraction, where one adorable giggle made Max forget what he was doing. And her most powerful move? The Super Snuggle Attack, where she would wrap her tiny arms around Max, instantly making him forget about all her mischievous ninja tricks.

One evening, as Max lay in bed, he heard tiny noises coming from Sophie's crib. He tiptoed closer and peeked in. Sophie was awake, rolling onto her tummy and practicing her ninja moves even while asleep. Max smiled and whispered, "Goodnight, Sneaky Baby Ninja."

Sophie might be small, but she was the Sneaky Baby Ninja—and Max was proud to be her big brother.

12: The Best Big Brother Award

Walter burst into the house, slamming the door so loudly that the picture with the cat on the wall jumped. In his hands, he was clutching a shiny gold medal with the inscription "Skipping Rope Master 2025," which he had just won at a school competition.

- Mom, Dad, look, I won! He cried, running into the living room.

His fair hair was messy from the wind, and his face had a triumphant smile. But before he could show his prize, something small and quick rushed to his feet. It was his little sister, Mary - a one-year-old torpedo with curls and handles, sticky with juice.

"Gu-gu-da!" Mary squealed, grabbing his knees and trying to climb him like a tree. Walter staggered and dropped the medal, which rolled under the couch. - Oh no, Mary, you again! He groaned, crouching down to peel it off. Mom came in with a plate of sandwiches, and Dad glanced over the newspaper.

- Walter, congratulations! - said my mother.
"But it looks like Mary wants to celebrate with you."

"Rather, she ruins my victory parade," muttered Walter, reaching under the couch for the medal. Mary grabbed his sleeve and began to pull it, guggling: "Ba-da-ga!".

Walter sighed, picked up the medal and sat down on the carpet to free himself.

"You know what, Mary?" He said, showing her the glittering prize.

"This is for being the best at skipping rope. And they don't give medals for being an older brother, although I should get one, because I'm always watching you! Mary squealed and grabbed the medal, drooling it right away. "

"Hey, don't eat this!" Walter shouted, snatching him from her hands.

Dad laughed. "There may not be medals for being a brother, but you do it great. Mary adores you.

"Sure, she loves to smash my life," Walter grumbled, wiping the medal on his sweatshirt.

"Yesterday she threw down my blocks, the day before yesterday she lost my pencil, and now she's drooling over my prize!"

Mom put the plate on the table and sat down next to it.

- Walter, being an older brother is a difficult job, but you don't need a medal to be a champion at it. See how she looks at you.

Walter glanced at Mary, who was stretching out her hands to him with a wide smile.

"Gu-gu!" She cried, as if to say:

"You're great, brother!" He sighed and lifted her to his knees.

"Okay, little one, but don't drool any more of the medal, okay?" He said, and she grabbed his finger and started waving it like a baton.

Then he came up with an idea.

"Wait, what if I make my own prize?" - he called, jumping down on the carpet with Mary. He ran to his room, grabbed a piece of paper, crayons and duct tape. He sat down at the table and began to draw - a big, golden star with the inscription "Best Older Brother". Mary crawled behind him and climbed into a chair, trying to grab the crayon.

"Oh no, you little monster, this is my mission!" Walter laughed, giving her a blank sheet of paper to scribble. He made a star, cut it out and taped it to his sweatshirt.

"Look, this is my reward!" - he announced, standing in the pose of a winner.

Mom clapped her hands.
- Walter, it's brilliant! You are a champion and without a medal.
Dad nodded. "But you know, a real reward is more than a star on paper."

"What?" Walter asked, raising an eyebrow.

Before Dad could answer, Mary threw herself at Walter with force, knocking him over onto the carpet.

- Ba-da-da! She snapped, climbing up on his stomach and squeezing him with her hands. Walter squealed, pretending to defend himself.

"Okay, baby, love attack!" He called out and then grabbed her and held her up high as if she were a goblet.

"Okay, you're my living prize!" - he laughed, and Mary clapped her hands as if she was really celebrating.

For the rest of the afternoon, Walter played with Mary, inventing "missions for the best brother". First, he built her a track out of pillows so she could crawl on it - he called it the "Little Master Trail".

"If you pass, I'll get a point as a brother!" - he said, and Mary covered the route, knocking over one pillow and guggling triumphantly. Then they made a "skipping rope for two" - Walter was jumping, and Mary was waving her hands as if she was cheering him on. Once, he even let her hold the medal, making sure she didn't eat it.

"You're my assistant, little one," he joked, and she laughed as if she understood.

When it was time for dinner, Walter sat at the table with Mary on his lap.

"You know, Mom, Dad," he said, handing his sister a piece of bread,

I thought being a brother was just about keeping an eye on her and cleaning up after her. But it's also fun. I don't need a medal because I have it."

Mom smiled warmly. "That's the real reward, Walter—her love and the fact that you are important to her."

Dad nodded. "You are a master of skipping rope and a master of brotherhood. It's better than gold."

Walter looked at Mary, who grabbed his nose and blurted: "Gu-da!".

"Okay, little one, you're my best reward," he said, hugging her. His heart danced with pride and joy. Walter understood that being an older brother is not only about duties, but also joy - and that Mary's smile is worth more than all the medals in the world.

That night, Walter hung his paper star above his bed, next to a skipping rope medal.

"This is for you, Mary," he whispered, looking at his sister sleeping in the crib.

"You are my master, and I am your brother."

He fell asleep with a smile, knowing that the real prizes don't shine on the shelf, but they coo and cuddle every day.

From that day on, Walter was looking for ways to be the best brother. Sometimes he built castles from blocks for Mary, sometimes he jumped with her on his hands, pretending to be a kangaroo. His parents looked at him with pride, and he felt that every moment with his sister was a small win.

"You're in my team, little champion," he whispered to her before bedtime. And then he dreamed of new adventures in which they were always together - the best brother and his most valuable prize.

BEST
OLDER
BROTHER.

Part 4: Growing Together - A Lifelong Friendship

Growing Together -
a Lifelong Friendship

13: Teaching the Baby Something New

Mark was standing in the middle of the yard, balancing on one leg like a flamingo in a zoo. In his hands, he held two sticks, which he waved like an orchestra conductor, shouting, "Ta-da-da-dam!" I am the King of Balance!" The sun was reflected in the puddles after the morning rain, and the wind ruffled his dark hair. He had just come up with a new trick—jumping from one leg onto an old tire in the grass—when he suddenly heard the familiar "gu-gu!" behind him. He turned to see his little brother, Liam. crawling across the lawn straight at him, his face stained with juice and his eyes shining like flashlights.

"Liam, what are you doing here?" Mark cried, losing his balance and falling to the ground on both legs. Liam, a ten-month-old master of chaos, stopped at his brother's feet and stretched out his hands, fumbling: "Ba-da-ga!". Mark sighed.

"You're following me again, aren't you?" he said, smiling when he saw Liam trying to grab one of his sticks.

"Okay, little one, look at the Balance King!"

He returned to his pose, lifting his leg and waving his sticks.

"It's an art you won't learn so easily!"

Mom leaned out of the window of the house, carrying a basket of laundry.

"Mark, maybe you can show Liam something simpler?" She cried, laughing.

- He wants to be like you!- Like me? Mark muttered, raising an eyebrow.

- Then let him learn to walk first and not crawl like a turtle on a turbo! Dad, who was raking leaves next to the shed, laughed.

"Mark, you are his role model. He watches you and learns. Maybe you can think of something?"

Mark looked at Liam, who was now sitting on the grass and clapping his hands, as if he was cheering. "A pattern, you say?" - muttered.

"Okay, kid, I'll teach you something cool!"

He put down his sticks and crouched down in front of his brother.

"Watch and learn from the master!"

He started making silly faces: first he stuck out his tongue and narrowed his eyes like a frog, then puffed up his cheeks like a balloon.

- Boo! - he called, and Liam squealed with joy, waving his hands.

-See? It's easy! - said Mark, making another face - this time he pretended that his nose was running out of his face. Liam laughed so loudly that he rolled over on his back, gushing: "Ga-ga-da!". Mark stood up and nodded.

Well, not a bad student, but now something more challenging! He grabbed a stick, picked it up high, and pretended to play an invisible trumpet: 'Tu-tu-tu-tu-

tuuu!' Liam looked with delight, and then... He grabbed a small stone from the grass and lifted it up, letting out a quiet "tu-tu!"

Mark opened his mouth

. "Wait, what?!" -Cried.

"Are you imitating me, little one?!" - Liam repeated "tu-tu!" and waved the stone as if he was really playing the trumpet. Mark jumped with joy.

- Mom, Dad, look! Liam copies my trumpet! - Mom left the window, and Dad put down the rake and came closer.

"Come on, Mark, you're a teacher!" Dad said, clapping his hands.

"It's magic!" - Mark called, grabbing the second stick.

- Okay, Liam, now we're playing together! - He started to trumpet: 'Tu-tu-tu-tuuu!', and Liam picked up his stone and blurted: 'Tu-tu!' in the same rhythm. They looked like a small orchestra in the yard - Mark jumped and waved a stick, and Liam crawled behind him, trumpeting his "tu-tu!".

Mom ran out of the house with her phone, recording them.

"You guys are amazing!" She laughed.

But Mark did not want to stop there.

"Wait, Liam, I'll teach you one more trick!" - said.

He sat down on the grass, stretched out his arms and started pretending to catch invisible balls: "Hop, hop, I caught it!". Liam looked for a moment, and then... he stretched his arms and squealed: "Hop!" - as if he had also caught something. Mark jumped.

"He does! -Shouted.

- "Liam, you are brilliant! He grabbed his brother by the armpits and lifted him high. You're my little follower!"

For the rest of the afternoon, Mark was coming up with new things to teach Liam. He showed him how to stamp his feet to the rhythm

- "Thump, thump, thump!" - and Liam slapped his hands on the grass, exclaiming: "Thump, thump!" Then he pretended to fly like a bird, waving his hands - "Flap, flap!" - and Liam spread his hands and shouted: "Fa-fa!". Once, Mark fell on the grass, pretending to fall with a bang - "Boom!" - and Liam threw himself on his stomach and squealed: "Boom!". Mom and Dad watched from the bench, laughing and taking pictures.

- Mark, you are an absolute master of teaching! - said Dad.

When the sun began to set, Mark sat next to Liam on a blanket under an apple tree.

"You know what, kid?" He said, handing him a piece of apple.

"You're quick to learn, and I'm your role model. It's cool, even when we do stupid things!" - Liam blurted, "Ba-da!" and grabbed the apple, then stretched out his hand and patted Mark on the nose, as if to say, "Thanks, brother!"

That night, Mark drew a poster—a large shield with the inscription "Mark and Liam—A Team of Followers." He drew himself with a stick-trumpet and Liam with a stone and then hung the poster above his bed.

"Liam, you learn from me, and I learn from you," he whispered, looking at his brother sleeping in the crib.

"Being your role model is like magic. "

A proud smile crept across his face, impossible to hide.

Mark understood that showing Liam the world - even the most mundane things - was something great, because the little one looked at him as a hero.

From that day on, Mark played the role of Liam's teacher.

He taught him to wave "bye, bye," peek-a-boo, and even knock on the table like a drum. Liam imitated him with a smile, sometimes adding his own "gu-gu!" to each trick. His parents laughed when they saw Mark showing his brother more and more new things.

"You're his first master, Mark," his mother said.

Mark answered: "And he is mine, because he teaches me patience!"

He fell asleep with pride, dreaming about more lessons for his little follower, knowing that being a role model is the best adventure.

14: The Great Diaper Disaster

Henry was sitting on the carpet in the living room, surrounded by his beloved robot figurines. He was putting the Robot Warrior in an epic pose, ready to fight the Space Monster, when he suddenly heard a suspicious sound - something like a silent explosion and then a giggle. He raised his head and saw his little brother, George, sitting in a car seat a few steps away. George was nine months old, his face smeared with apple mousse and his hands stretched out towards Henry, as if he was calling for help. But it wasn't the mousse that was the problem - there was a smell wafting from the car seat, which made Henry wrinkle his nose and squeal:

"Oh no, George, again?!"

- Mom, Dad, George made a bomb in his diaper! He cried, jumping to his feet and running to the kitchen, where his mother was cutting vegetables for dinner. His blond hair was bouncing, and he was already making an escape plan in his head. Mom turned around with a knife in her hand and smiled.

- Henry, it's just a diaper. Can you help me?

- Help?! - shouted Henry, stopping in the doorway.

"It smells like a garbage factory! Why does he need so many diapers?"

Dad came in from the garden carrying a bucket of soil.

"Because he's small, Henry," he said, laughing.

"But if you help, you'll learn survival strategies!"

Henry rolled his eyes and returned to the living room, holding his nose. George blurted: "Ba-da-gu!" and waved his hands as if he was inviting his brother to play. "You little stinkop-maker," muttered Henry, looking at him from a distance.

"Okay, I'll do it, but I need a plan!"

He ran to his room, grabbed a scarf, tied it around his face like a ninja mask, and grabbed a wooden spoon as a 'protective weapon.' - Operation Diaper start! He cried, returning to the living room in full gear.

My mother was already waiting with a pack of diapers and wipes. "Henry, you look like a superhero," she laughed, putting George on the changing table.

"Hold his legs and I'll do the rest."

Henry approached carefully, raising the spoon like a shield. "Okay, George, no tricks!" He said, grabbing his brother's ankles. But before his mother could take off his diaper, George swung his legs like a fan, and Henry felt something wet land on his hand. "Yuck, a wet bomb attack!" He shouted, letting go of his legs and jumping away. Mum burst out laughing, and George muttered triumphantly: "Gu-ga-da!".

"It's a disaster!" - groaned Henry, wiping his hand on the scarf.

"Why can't he crawl by himself?"

Dad sat down on the couch, still laughing.

- Henry, he's too small. He needs us - and you - to help him. It's part of being a brother.

Henry wrinkled his nose. "But it stinks! And it is... yucky!"

He looked at George, who was now lying quietly, looking at him with a smile as if nothing had happened.

Mom changed George in record time and picked him up, clean and smelling of tissues. "See, Henry?" It's not so scary when you help," she said, handing him her brother.

Henry reluctantly took George in his arms, still holding the scarf over his face.

"Okay, kid, you're clean, but no more bombs, okay?" - he said, and George grabbed him by the nose and blurted: "Ba-da!".

Then Henry came up with an idea.

"Wait, I'll make an adventure out of this!" - cried. He put George on the carpet and ran to get a piece of paper and crayons. He drew a large map with the inscription "Diaper Mission" - the kitchen was "The Handkerchief Base", the living room was "The Battlefield", and his room was "Superbrother's Hideout". "George, you are my partner in this mission," he said, showing him the map. "But if you make another bomb, I'll run away, and you'll fight alone!" Mom smiled.

"Henry, it's a great way to deal with it." Dad nodded. "And it shows that you have empathy - you help, even though you don't like messes."

For the rest of the day, Henry turned every diaper disaster into a game. When George "exploded" again after dinner, Henry announced: "Attack of the Stink monster!" and ran to get the scarf, pretending to be a ninja on a mission. He was holding his brother's legs, and his mother was changing diapers, and he was making faces as if he were fighting a cosmic enemy.

"Phew, we've defeated the beast!" - he shouted when George was clean. Once, he even brought a diaper himself, waving his spoon like a sword.

"Go to battle, Handkerchief Base!" - he shouted, and George laughed as if he understood the joke.

In the evening, when George fell asleep in his cot, Henry sat down at the table with a plate of sandwiches.

You know, Mom, Dad," he said, biting his bread, "these diapers are terrible, but George is small, and he can't do anything about it. Helping him is like a superhero mission."

His mother hugged him. - Henry, this is called empathy. You understand what he needs, and you help, although you don't always like it. Dad nodded.

"And escaping with a scarf is a clever strategy. You are a master of survival!

Henry looked at the sleeping George and smiled. "Okay, little stinco-maker, I can be your super brother," he whispered.

But if you attack me again, I have a plan to retreat!" Hi walked away with pride in every step. Henry understood that helping his brother, even in such yucky moments, was important, because empathy means support and sometimes also a quick escape from the battlefield.

That night, Henry drew a badge - a shield with the inscription "Hero of Diaper Missions" and a dragon (George) inside. He hung it over the bed and whispered,

"You're in my team, little one." But next time, I'll take a gas mask! He fell asleep with a smile, dreaming of new strategies for diaper disasters, knowing that being a brother was sometimes a dirty job - but worth the effort. From that day on, Henry approached diaper missions with humor. Sometimes, he put on a scarf, and sometimes, he pretended to run away from the "bomb," but he always helped because he knew that George needed him. His parents laughed at his tricks, and he felt like a hero—even with a wet hand.

"You're my stink-partner, George," he whispered before bedtime. And then he planned further adventures in which empathy and laughter always won.

Diaper Mission

15: Forever Teammates

Robert burst into the house, throwing his backpack on the floor with such a bang that the clock on the wall trembled. He was holding a football in his hands, dirty with mud after today's match, and he had a smile on his face from ear to ear.

- Mom, Dad, I scored a goal!

He cried, running into the living room. His blond hair was wet with sweat, and his knees were covered with grass. But before he could tell about his victory, something small and quick grabbed his leg. It was his little sister, Mia - a one-year-old sprinter on all fours, with curls bouncing like springs and arms stretched out towards the ball.

"Gu-gu-da!" - squealed Mia, trying to climb his leg like a ladder. Robert staggered and dropped the ball, which rolled under the table.

- Oh no, Mia, not now! He groaned, crouching down to peel it off.

Mom came in from the kitchen carrying a plate of apples, and dad scolded from behind a newspaper on the couch. - Robert, bravo for the goal! - said dad.

"But it looks like Mia wants to be part of your team." Robert muttered, picking up the ball and wiping it on his pants. Mia blurted: "Ba-da!" and followed him, dragging a stuffed rabbit behind her.

Robert sat down on the carpet, holding the ball out of her reach.

"You know what, Mia?" He said, looking at her. "You're small and you drool all the time, but one day you'll stop being that little one. What then?"

Mia stretched out her hands as if she wanted to catch the ball, and Robert smiled.

"Maybe one day we'll play soccer together?" He said jokingly, but a spark lit up in his head.

Mom put the plate on the table and sat down next to it.

"Robert, she's growing faster than you think," she said.

"Sure, close to my ball," Robert grumbled, but he picked up the rabbit and waved it in front of her face. "Gu-gu!" She cried, grabbing the toy and squeezing it with a smile. Dad put the newspaper down.

"You're a team, Robert. Now you are guarding it, and one day you will run around the field together."

Robert looked at Mia and frowned

. -Team? -Muttered.

"Okay, baby, we're going to make you my teammate!" He got up, caught the ball and started tossing it. "Watch and learn from the captain!" He said, kicking the ball slightly towards the carpet. Mia squealed and followed it on all fours, trying to catch it. Robert laughed.

"Okay, you're fast, but you still need to practice!"

Then he came up with an idea.

"Wait, we're going to do a team training!" He cried, running to his room. He came back with a piece of paper, crayons and an old string. He drew a poster with the inscription "Robert and Mia - Eternal Teammates" - at the top, it was with a ball, and at the bottom, Mia was with a rabbit. He stuck the string as a "medal" and hung the poster on the wall.

- It's our contract, Mia! He said, sitting down next to her. "Now we train together, but no saliva on my ball, right? Mia blurted out: "Da-ga!" and caught the ball, drooling it right away. Robert rolled his eyes, but laughed.

"Okay, one point for you, little one!"

For the rest of the afternoon, Robert played with Mia, building their "team". First, he set up a track made of pillows - "Playground for Toddlers" - and helped her crawl after the ball, shouting: "Kick, Mia, kick!". She was rolling the ball with her hands, and Robert was pretending it was a goal, jumping and shouting:

"Bravo, teammate!".

Then they took a "penalty kick" - Robert threw the ball on the blanket, and Mia caught it with a rabbit, laughing when it landed on her head. Once, he even sat on the carpet himself and let her kick the ball with his legs, pretending to be a goalkeeper.

"Defended!" - he shouted, and Mia clapped her hands.

Mom and Dad looked on with a smile.

"Robert, you're captain of the year," Mom said, taking the picture.

"You're eternal teammates," Dad added.

"She's growing, and you're showing her the world. " Robert looked at Mia, who was now sitting on a blanket waving the rabbit.

"You know, little one," he said quietly, "one day you'll stop being a toddler." You'll walk, run, maybe even score a goal. And then what?" - Mia blurted out: "Gu-da!" and stretched out her hand, as if to give a high five. Robert grabbed her hand and shook it.

"Okay, we'll always be a team," he laughed.

In the evening, when Mia fell asleep in her crib, Robert sat down at the table with a sandwich in his hand. "Mom, Dad," he said, chewing on his bread,

"I thought being a brother was just about keeping an eye on her and cleaning up the mess. But it's also about teaching her cool things. She will grow up one day, and I will be her captain." Mom smiled.

"Robert, you are right. You grow together, and you give her a start." Dad nodded.

"And you'll always be a teammate - even when you grow up."

Robert looked at sleeping Mia and his eyes lit up with pride after hearing the praise.

"You're my little player, Mia," he whispered. "Now you're crawling after my ball, but we'll run together one day. He stood up and adjusted the poster on the wall, adding a small crown over Mia's head. "Eternal Teammates," he muttered with a smile.

That night, Robert fell asleep, dreaming of the future—of Mia, who no longer crawls but runs around the pitch kicking a ball. He stands next to her, shouting, "Come on, teammate!" He imagines him teaching her tricks, winning games together, and then laughing back at the days she drooled over his ball. He knows that Mia will not be a toddler forever but will always be his best friend—a team for life.

From that day on, Robert looked at Mia as a partner in an adventure. He taught her to knock the ball over, wave "bye, bye", and sometimes sit with her on a blanket, talking about his goals. His parents laughed when they saw him building a bond with her.

"You're in my team, little one," he whispered to her before bedtime. And then he'd fall asleep, knowing that even though time was running out, their team would never fall apart—because real teammates stick together forever.

We'd love to hear your thoughts!

If you enjoyed this book, we would appreciate it if you could leave a review.

Your feedback means a lot and helps other readers discover our stories.

Kick Mia
Kick!

A Letter from the Big Brother Club

To our newest member...............

Dear Big Brother,
Welcome to the Big Brother Club!

You've just joined the most amazing, important, and sometimes slightly sticky adventure in the world – becoming an older sibling. That's right. From now on, you're a superhero in someone's eyes (even if they can't say it yet).

Here are a few things you should know:

✓ You're their first best friend.
✓ You're their guide to all things fun.
✓ You're the only one who knows how to make them giggle in the middle of a diaper disaster.

Your mission?

To be kind. To be patient. To be silly. To protect your little sibling from broccoli.
(Yes, that's a real rule. We checked.)
We've heard great things about you already – and we're so glad to have you on our team.
Keep up the good work, and remember: even the smallest moments (like a high five or a funny face) can be the start of a big adventure.

Signed,
The Big Brother Club

P.S. If your little sibling drools on your stuff...
it means they love you. Probably.

Made in United States
Cleveland, OH
25 May 2026

37377992R00085